THE OUTER WARDS

The Outer Wards

SADIQA DE MEIJER

THE POETRY IMPRINT AT VÉHICULE PRESS

Published with the generous assistance of the Canada Council for the
Arts and the Canada Book Fund of the Department of
Canadian Heritage.

 Canada Council Conseil des arts
for the Arts du Canada   Canadä

SIGNAL EDITIONS EDITOR: CARMINE STARNINO

Cover design by David Drummond
Photo of the author by Cat London
Set in Minion and Filosofia by Simon Garamond
Printed by Marquis Book Printing Inc.

Dépôt légal, Library and Archives Canada and the
Bibliothèque national du Québec, second trimester 2020.

LIBRARY AND ARCHIVES CANADA CATALOGUING IN PUBLICATION

Title: The outer wards / Sadiqa de Meijer.
Names: De Meijer, Sadiqa, 1977- author.
Description: Poems.
Identifiers: Canadiana (print) 20190227591 | Canadiana (ebook)
20190227605 | ISBN 9781550655452 (softcover)
ISBN 9781550655513 (HTML)
Classification: LCC PS8607.E4822 O98 2020 | DDC C811/.6—dc23

Published by Véhicule Press, Montréal, Québec, Canada
www.vehiculepress.com

Distribution in Canada by LitDistCo
www.litdistco.ca

Distributed in the U.S. by Independent Publishers Group
www.ipgbook.com

Printed in Canada

voor mijn moeder

I am flushed and warm.
I think I may be enormous,
I am so stupidly happy,
My Wellingtons
Squelching and squelching through the beautiful red.

–SYLVIA PLATH, 'Letter in November'

Time to plant tears, says the almanac.

–ELIZABETH BISHOP, 'Sestina'

CONTENTS

On Origins

Spoon, spoon

I, too, have a small version

I had one made
in the meticulous workshop
under my navel

They started with a fish,
then frog, then rabbit

And I asked them to stop at human

Like you, we are head over heels
when we look at each other

We go to sleep
concave, convex
in the room's particulate dark

Because I would know what to do
with a cranium slowly
gathering doubt

Goodnight nobody, goodnight mush

Mornings, we're sprawled
as if marooned

Bind

Adorable remora,
you skew my velocities.
Phlebologist in a white onesie,
draining my corpuscles drowsily, remorseless.
Now you speak in your gorgeous distortions,
forms below the water's flowing lens.
When you're with me, my attention
is your nourishment, its remnant
molecules diffusing in the murk.
When you're not, I wear the imprint
of your absence like a bruise.

Mother of Vinegar

Observe her, forming
low in the flask, gelatinous
and tentacled, like a clot
of that blood
I said it doesn't hurt to lose.

The curse. The rag. Earth's maw
collecting windfall thuds. The bruised substance
sours, collapses the tongue.

We wear the apples, rotten little skulls,
strung around our necks.

Woolgather, withdraw.
Cloaked in brine, in mineral decay.

Cramps are its motion, inward, folding
the latest parachute.

I am telling you of a miracle.
The moon brews it, and we sluice it out.

Leaves you clean as gin.
The greatest thing I ever did,
this was my material.

Incantation

Cider light of spring
perforates the maples—

they bloom in tight vermilion packets
that the squirrels chew, discard.

Fabric of small aggregates of families,
pushbikes, buckets, stuffies.

Single thunder of the metal slide undenting.
The mothers clutch coffees, they wave and relate.

I'm not quite right.
One hand pushes the swing, the other holds an open book,

paper valley of an elsewhere.
And an axe, Kafka said—

love, I recalibrated all catastrophes
when you were born,

and they were worse—
the sloping lines, I read

in gulps, while automatically repeating
wheeeeeee

as you fly elliptically out
of my attention, which should be undivided, but is

skulking for the possibility
that words

could suddenly align the elements—
then every gesture

has a choreography: rope climber in its tilted
orbit, woman emptying

a shoe of sand, fledgling
robin's skimming flight—and I'm

forgiven, bookish, motherly, because the weave,
made visible, leaves nothing out,

not even you, not even me.

Reading dèr Mouw After Bedtime

Star light, star bright, first star I see tonight.
Everything comes too late, he wrote of a woolen bunny,
during The War to End All Wars.

So I suddenly adore her when she sleeps,
and plummets inward, fish-mouthed, grip releasing
a clutched what?

Wash the dishes, wipe the dishes, ring the bell for tea.
I'm Brahman, but we are without a maid, he also wrote.
The glass eyes of her animals are on me, mute tribunal.

There is no nothing because even air
is air, she'd said. I almost violently wanted her to eat some
   more.
Then I wished for the nothing her hand had grasped.
And the war was supposed to end war.

Women Do This Every Day

At the park I look for Levita,
because our work is the same—
swaying wide-legged over foraging toddlers,
we avert bruises, discourage the consumption
of found objects, interpret primordial languages,
serve fruit from hastily filled containers,
and trade a few stories and questions, so I know

that it's not the same work,
because the toddler is her employer's,
and evenings she goes to a small apartment, crammed with
      roommates
who are also working thousands of kilometers from home,
and she tells me of a mountain farm, and shrimp paste, and her wish
for dental work, and we laugh, having the same missing molar,
and I tell her about camping, and I never think to ask if she has
      children,
because I still underestimate the violence,

but they are six and three she says one morning,
early in the fall when we are waving wasps from the cut apples,
and the youngest doesn't remember her, and then she takes my dismay
for condemnation, and says furiously *they are not like children here,
the older one can cook, the little one can sweep,*
and my girl wants to nurse, and I'm apologizing senselessly
for everything I ever haven't done.

The Roaring Alongside

The school's so close, some mornings
when I hang the laundry, that I hear her name
—now here, now there—in the cacophony
of voices, like dings of toy cash registers.
That means she is it in tag.

And I was trusted, somewhere in the April firmament.
Shaking the damp, corkscrewed fabrics out;
husks of a small human, sapling slender,
thinned in the knees.

I'd emptied her pockets. Everything I'd ever said to her
was in them, turned to sand. *The millions of grains are black, white,*
*   tan, and gray,*
mixed with quartz grains, rose and amethyst.

Provisions

Veering round aisle corners, tilt of the cart's
pot-bellied heft—her comma legs poke through the gaps,
we whisk past bins, her laugh is the birth of all roses. Pitched
sideswipe of a chips display, I've never
elated anyone

as much as her inside our headlong now.
I want to buttonhole the other shoppers,
who are grim and preoccupied,
reaching for cereal—

people, you're going to be dead!

I sober up in Organics;
deliberate sunscreens, purchase the least
carcinogenic, then can't afford the proper flour
for the proper bread.

It's the Inner Harbour neighbourhood, but everyone calls it Skeleton Park

My daughter holds two of my fingers in her fist.
Cheerfully greets everything but people:
hello there, snail, hello tulip, hi paper cup!

At the chestnut tree, I always lift her into the branches,
and repeat a rhyme in my own language.

Margaret on the corner keeps trinkets on the window sill.
The house was her father's shoe repair shop. She sits out front
in her lawn chair, sunburned, older than electric blankets. If you
    admire
anything, she gives it to you. She asked me once to chase
a scary bird from her cellar. When I feel spectral,
the unmodulated volume of her greeting
gives me form.

The lilacs are primordial perfumeries.

A duck leaves a strangely long wake in the park grass, parting,
    parting—
wait, it's ducklings!

Mama, let's pretend that I'm a stranger to this land,
and I don't even know what the sky is.

The closest I've come
to holding the chirps and warbles of her voice
was when she sang to me through a pool noodle,
and each word trilled in my hands.
I wanted it to last forever.

Aphids on the milkweed pods: ochre, powdery roe. When she finds
        ladybugs,
she delivers them to their sustenance.

I've never looked at the back of my hand as intently
as we have examined this street.

An idling car is a consciousness.

That hollow between the sidewalk segments
is called wish world; you have to drop
a flower in it when you pass.

Dandelions and earthworms weren't here, earlier.

From one yard comes a cough that is a grievance. *Do you think
an ogre lives there*, she whispers.

Near The Store Famous
is an aperture where summer enters
the neighbourhood. We're willingly barefoot.
I carry her over the blistering tarmac.

The meows of Tyra the tortoise shell cat sound like the word hello.

s in a chair on his sloped lawn, belligerent
unless Portugal wins. He has railed against Pakistanis
on my own porch, and been sent away, and returned
with lovage and lettuce from his garden, because he is twofold
like everyone else, fluctuant between a face and an idea. At her
lemonade stand, he hands her five dollars
and says *no drink, I've got the sugar.*

Dead squirrel's eye is a burnt currant—
she pokes its tummy with a stick.
What made it dead?

We see Helen, and she's pregnant. Soon she'll be with us
in this submerged world.

A tug on my pants means lift me.

She presses her hands to her ears, against the pervasive
hammering, sawing—that's the gentry, making their houses
over. I am part of it, but not enough.

Teenagers on longboards, gangly and mesmeric. The noise
of the wheels is a mantra.

We eat on the front steps, bowls of dal in our laps.
Overhead, nature is stripping the paint for me.

Also, the light on one of Gus's windows, at sunrise,
makes rows of golden yellow squares for a few minutes,
then abruptly goes.

She climbs the cannon at the park's edge. I promise to catch her
when she leaps. Silently, I hold the images of my century;
violence on the scale of metal balls is quaint.
At downpours, we stand in the street's shallow river,
make currents in the gritty water with our toes.

I'm foreign, and she is home.

The lake is a banner without a slogan, strung between the houses.
We smell it, the odd morning; a lithic clarity with an edge of fish.

Wad of filthy tissues at her feet—*don't touch!*—but I get closer,
it's a rust-edged peony.

We wave at Leah, who coasts downhill on her bike
after a night shift in obstetrics. While we slept, was she the first
human that someone ever saw? Her face is right for it,
a kind moon.

Pedestrians carry laptop bags, or groceries, or take-out, or they tug
at a leash and ask if my daughter wants to pet their dog
who is friendly. She does.

Lord, some days there's so much whiteness, hard
as the stratified walls of old quarries that edge the backyards.
I'm Guatemalan, Native, Arabic, whatever, they insist they've met
my sister, but I have no sister. And the ones who say,
that's so interesting, I'm just boring old nothing, are the most
dangerous people, who think they have no history.

When we meander, slowly, nowhere,
all my places are in my pocket.

During the dog days, the roads are still. People have siphoned
to cottages. At the splashpad, small rainbows
and wilting parents.

Evening's relief. The tree receives a great wind.

She sprints after wild rabbits at dusk, seeking to hold them.
When I catch one, can we keep it? I say sure,
because of the odds.

On the sidewalk is a man weaving a low bike around the bins,
eyes ticking between alleys, porches, people
whom I don't expect to recognize, because even if I say hello,
I segregate and think of it as vigilance—
he sees a whole different neighbourhood. I'd like to ask,
but we don't even speak much alike.

Rumours of meteor showers. Too much urban light.

When Sei practices marimba with the window open, we sit
on a stump in her yard to listen. I saw her perform at the church
with the apparition of her father.

There's a woman perpetually at an upper window
in the nursing home who waves at us. One day she is
at the doors in a wheelchair, and presents
markers and a colouring book.

Mama, what made myself?

When the road is dug up for sewer repairs, it turns out
that Margaret has been sitting, in her lawn chair,
along an ancient, subterranean river.

That small maple is the first to turn each year; an ignition
in the crown.

Once I used to go to movies. She has to pee, and I recall
the Kiarostami title, 'Where is the friend's home?' Our luck here
is that around every corner, there is a friend's home.

Mama, I am going to bless you because I see a ragweed.

She loves to swing in the playground on the ossuary,
where only the Irish and Scottish have plaques.
I start to tell her of the bones under the bones—
but Brandon's no ghost, crossing the park in skinny jeans,
humming his two-spirit self into being.

Then the months enter a chute, strung with rituals.

A clear day is for collecting leaves to dip in beeswax.
She's indiscriminate. *Mama, why didn't you
pick that one up?* I inspect the torn, brown scrap,
and see the strictures of my aesthetic.

A crowd of starlings descends on an apple tree.
They poke at the soft, copper spheres,
then seem a little drunk.

One night, everyone is their other selves, costumed,
in the center of the park. It frightens her.

She says she loves me more than fifty-four-a-hundred. I say love
has no measurements, there is enough in the world
for everything. *Everything? I didn't know that,* she answers,
and turns quiet. *Even concrete?* I feel compelled
to sustain the premise with a yes.
How does concrete cry?

The spindle reveries of trees are flecked with nests,
small clots of thought.

We scrape out a turnip, place a tealight, sing *I'm walking
with my lantern, my lantern walks with me.*

I move differently now, which means I have altered
my temporal experience. My tread is gradual, and my mind
is an umbrella. I know the minutes as the lichens
on the breakwater know them. It is like holding my usual breath
for a few years, and finding that another part
of me is breathing.

The houses get draped in lights, some a frigid, diode blue.
Then there are singers at the door, and she hides behind me,
listens with all her ears.

I pull her on the sled. Some days we don't get far, because
every snowbank is a place to disembark and throw herself
into its cushion. On others, we make it to the grocery store
and she rides home hugging coffee and oats.

Cars slide past the stop sign.

She loves to eat the snow, so I impose a new rule: graze only
from shrubs and trees.

The playground is forlorn, except for the crows. The slides
are magnificently fast. Alone, I prefer to avoid the park
after midnight or so. That conversation,
when she's older, will fracture this living map
that we're making
again.

To patch the torn knees of her snowsuit, I cut two bright hearts
out of an old shopping bag, and pad them with scraps of wool
while watching 'The Office.' In the morning,
she is pleased.

From the top of Patrick Street, the neighbourhood
looks like a painting; faint brushstrokes, colours of stones.

The whack of the puck on the boards of the park rink is discrete
and vacuous, as if it occurs in outer space.

Our mittens hold hands while she stomps the milk-white
ice of the puddles to shards.

Deep within every landscape,
something is in bloom.

Shut-In

Mr. Hubble, it turns out the universe shrinks
to a sore bed, thumb-screwed skull,
curtains doubled for darkness,
panic pressing in.
I am the broken mechanism,
hold the only record of the crash, interrogate
myself relentlessly, futile reconstruction,
until at last they are home.
Creaks, voices, onions frying in oil. A song erupts
and my brain impales on the jagged blade of its tune—
then a hushing, *quiet for mama, quiet for mama!*—
somehow I'm still too big. The house
has an impossible foundation,
glows under dimming skies, a candled egg. Someone
raises it to their enormous eye.

The Imaging Department

Why was the clock in a cage?
There should have been whistles and sweat,
a floor the colour of North Atlantic storms, lines of a subway map–
but it wasn't a gym. The air had wavelengths, a synthetic lemon smell.
We were on the same side, everyone for themselves.
Were we dangerous, would we rage at it?
We held the coffee cups with trap door lids.
Someone's sneaker blankly tapped the air.

Half of the colon and most of a lung, is what one woman's husband
had removed. Their son said, *You're half empty space.*
This was now; they eyed their flat phones.
The father could have risen like a thick balloon, quietly thudding
the ceiling, smiling shy licorice teeth.

A woman in pastels came in. *I'm going to butcher this name*, she said,
so I stood. She led me to the table where they'd view
that clockwork part of me. *Lie still, real still.*
They started the cold IV. I'd read of a man who, during his lethal
    injection,
jerked up three times to say, *It don't work.*

And wanting not to think of him, I studied the ceiling's
print of hands, naïve and bright. So someone had been there,
attempting a signal, in this room of leaden aprons and electric noise,
radio reporting a larger city's traffic. Dear mother,
I wished you were my country again, when my ears didn't ring,

when my eyelids were still knitted shut—
and then I heard them say, *That's it*. When I turned
I saw it pulse in dark and grainy currents
on a screen. Nothing like a valentine
or dove—uncatalogued
marine, perhaps, and blunderous,
and fugitive.

How to Decline a Persistent Invitation

Yes, I'd love to, soon.
A question mark, a dial tone.
Her eyes are wide open, the midwife said—
that dark blue ink I drowned in.

Hang on, it won't be long.
Rustles in the wall, lost stitch.
The eyes, witch hazel, trusting. They used to drift,
agape at sunlight in the canopy.

Maybe later, love.
Night winds, felled tree.
Once, I saw them studiously replicate my blinking.
Now they grow a bird's transparent lids.

I can't say when.
Scrutiny, flowering borage. Where there's smoke.
They know the weather of my face,
the hole in my nightgown, the pill that's rolled under the bed.

Bear doesn't mind
if he drags on the ground,
or is smudged with glue, or forgotten
under the bed for a while,
paw stumps bearded with dust.
Lovingly covered with a worn quilt,
cradled as suckling, or slumped
on a chair as audience for an improvised epic
of trolls and robbers and one good fairy—
bear's single expression remains
and is kind; umber eyes and a stitched anchor mouth.

But I am that one;
I ate from the tree, and it hurt to give birth,
and was brilliant, giving birth,
and all my life I've cleaved
the possibilities
like that, and I don't regret, I don't regret
forcing myself to look.

Though when bear has been left
in my sight for the day, or I in his gaze,
while I dwell in my stale bed, exiled from an exile,
burning like coals with all I can't do,

then his mute, untroubled face, his eternal refusal
to be divided—I'm five or six years old,
and can remember flight. I don't mean
that I imagined or dreamed it; I was intimate
with the uplift in the belly, currents of the wind,
round crowns of trees and grids of shingles passing,
not that far

below, should I have fallen—and children do,
slowly, relentlessly,
in torrents of questions, in resin that holds
and lowers them.

I don't recall
an impact, but somehow I landed
at last in this bed, earthbound and alone,
wishing I could still speak the bear's language.

The darkness then was darker than we know;
it never left the corners of a room,
rose velvetly from cellars, where it blinded the potatoes—
like curd it formed a film on wooden spoons.

Grains of darkness clustered between brothers.
Dark moisture kept the cabbage leaves apart.
All over the old country, there were nights: no hands, no
    ground.
You've never really seen the stars.

And what was in it? Specters, wraiths—they spooked the horse.
Some things that people did.

A continent was dark. It could be what we wanted.

Animists, ivory, pith of strange fruits. We must have been,
for all intents, asleep.

When those nations flickered and were lit,
there was no fault to speak of.
And we didn't speak of it.

How to Take Meals in Semi-Darkness

Give thanks for this clock that still quarters the day.
Mutes the stupid jukebox in your skull

a while. Utensils have no bearing. Here is the silent offering,
here is a shadowed field on a tray: a leaf, a root, a hen?

Forms from the void, dim and earthly.
Dear Sputnik, trust the cook.

She asked me to look after *aapje*, her monkey.
To this I could say yes, while trapped in bed.
I can't attend your birthday, I later said
to its wide, narrow mouth, its eyes of impish dots—
this was good practice for the real face,
which had a cold, and was in class,
whistle-breathing, labouring over a backwards three.

On Violence

The schoolbuses come to the edge
of the park that's too small for a name, and hinge
their red appendages out,
damming the stream of commuters.

The children stagger up, sleepy armadillos.
Sunlight washes the narrow yards, opening crocuses,
pooling in the lenses of a broken pair of glasses.
And one little girl with a crook
in her neck, with a drag in her gait,
throwing rocks at the starlings,
dark flusters.

Who didn't throw rocks,
who didn't throw rocks,
who never used to throw rocks.

O, Death

Are you there,
in the long asphalt sigh of tires in the rain,
and under the bark of the old maples, eavesdropping,
smelling softly of pencil lead—

is it you who causes those small, metallic implosions
when the mail comes up the street?

You're the faint, falling bodies
of the midges, their plumed antennae,
their charcoal, undulant, funnelling swarms
over the shrubs at dusk.

You make such awkward entrances sometimes.

Or you leave the party and don't even tell anyone.
I've done it before.

And I've rigged games so I couldn't lose,
and found myself ugly and lonely.

You're the gravel sediment, and a vast thirst,
and a lock. The constellation of holes in the rice
when it's cooked. You want to hold us,
but you press too close.

You in rehearsal, or you on a rampage.
When water streams in contradicting currents to the grate,
its houndstooth ridges are your fleeting eyes.

Or are you always there, a cover of umber glass.
And you shatter, and then there's no air.

Paradise Found

And would I see them, then,
waiting at the arrivals gate,
straining through the stream of people
for me, anxious—would I know her
chapel posture and thick lenses,
and observe again the recognition
reach her face, a tidal bloom, the sturdy purse
of cough drops in her grip—and would she drive me
in her lurching old machine, to the deafened organist,
who practiced every evening grave galactic chords,
animate tremors in the floors and walls
of that dear house, its smell of rugs and soup,
and a ghostly matron shelling capucijners at the sink,
wiping her palms on her apron, naming my earliest name,
and that restless, generous uncle with his afro and visions,
     exhausted,
paint under his fingernails, handing me a V8?
(And even if I loved them
only on the pages, would Etty Hillesum
be pensive at her desk on the Museumplein—*But it is really
the other way round: heaven lives in me. Everything lives
in me*—and James Baldwin, having an elegant,
distracted smoke) and also Wouter, who said
no God, no afterlife, no war, and went to jail, and later
grew tomatoes in a rented square of earth,
regretting the blackbirds trapped
in the strawberry nets, his loaf hands cradling

the stunned parcels with their eye of panic,
that flapped lopsided to a shrub—Wouter,
who shook a little at the Ede station when we last parted—
and would he be alright, or still bleeding and bruised
from the way his bicycle landed?

On Faith

Move, mountain,
or I am no mother.

Matokie Lives

From that heaven I would take my leave.
I'd have such eerie, sublimating surfaces. A homing,
gravitational—I'd fall so vaporously
to the summit park, ground stowed with bones,
rope climber, scarred maple housing a screech owl, and the
    star
of tarmac streets that fractures out from there, I'd hurry
along the houses, seeking her,
clavicle, visceral imprint,

and finding that I couldn't intervene—the atom's
vacuum universe, the broken nerve—
nothing moving to my nothing hands, my ether tongue,
the neighbours' conversations undisturbable, the sidewalk
    chalk
inert in its box, and even calling mountainously
out to her, like willing consciousness into a dream,
while she puts the lego person on the horse,
and doesn't raise her eyes, and doesn't pause;
I'd have to ache and let her life unfold,

which is the greatest form of love,
I've read, if you can stomach it, from colic
to Wounded Knee—I never could, I'd have to name
a surrogate, who might be somewhere on another street,
weeding cabbages, humming a tune. I'd try to speak to them,
wanting to sound oracular, raising my rounded wings—
you on the stage, you who can trouble the water—

and when there was no answer, I would rain on them
the only currency remaining,
meaning rain.

The Outer Wards

I saw that I would have to cross the river,
and that it was the Rijn.
I had a fox, a goose, a sack of grain.

I said, I love the gay men in kufiyas on the Rembrandtplein,
and the muted half of me, from a land of five converging waters,
with an upstream alphabet—
so what makes me yours
every night, slow current, floodplain
of drowning grass?

Then the goose was in the reeds. It had an egg.
Twigs and quills, the ruckus of two pulses.
The grain had blown into my field. Someone was claiming it.
And the fox was a vanishing streak.

I could take my name, but not my papers.
I could take the swept air, but not my breath,
or not in one load. My promises, but not the child
I'd made them to, unless I could bring something back—
but the weather, the barges, the clouds turning orange and rose.

That Last Ferry

I've practiced the crossing enough
on this earth, have I not?
And willingly, finding it beautiful even—

the dory, docked on the inlet's sluggish pulse,
goes to Polruan. Sweater of cable-knit porridge.
Hello's a narrowing of one eye, the other's on the tide.
The boat holds two bicycles and three people,
or seven people, or a woman and all her belongings,
even her stage fright, her *tawiz*.
Hoarse blackback gulls gash the sky's graphite fabric.
Local boys daydream of shooting them.

Then that leviathan ship,
the crews hang on platforms to whitewash, whitewash—
it swallowed a road, a passenger train.
Sticky plastic cubes in the daycare. Turnstiles,
a duty-free liquor store, grid of ochre bottles
refracting porthole light. Freighters are weak signals
on the sea's living radar. Crescent of a sleeping man
in a lifeboat, maybe he has no papers.
We leave a brute and fissured wake that will
later lap a coastal marsh,
quietly at oyster amplitudes—

what else will I fail to perceive? As children,
waiting for the metal boat that, quarter of an hourly,

draws its liquid, dispersing ellipsis
on the river's mercurial skin. 'No swimming' sign,
black dot for a head. The right of way goes to barges,
their names please our mouths:
Victorie, Alina, Grunwald. Bikes strewn on the slope,
we feed the Flemish Giants clover. Goats tethered
to stakes in the grass. *They eat anything,* the farmer says,
even tins! I'm too shy to ask her, why don't they eat the rope?
Rectangle pupils. That glacially flattened landscape
in my mother's sunglasses.

Or in love on the Pacific straits. The crowd's
restrained, Brittanic stampede for good seats—
we cradle coffees, trade the camera, but I don't seek
an image, I want my hands to see: curls brown as grain,
the shoulders' heft—wayward praises
that the engine and the wind swallow. A lull
between islands, Edenic surplus
of life: bald eagles, seals, porpoises, strange ducks,
purple starfish on the rocks, and bull kelp
with its bladders and its tails—an almost scripture
billows in the waves,

and once, alone in a rain suit, turning a wheel
to pull that yellow platform on a cable
over the Lende, reed beds
shrieking with birds. Familiar land under clouds
of grim warning. I was holding
an old plastic bag with a clutch of nettles
for spring tonics,

and is that what still frightens me
at this hour,
unsalvageable
in this blanketed vessel,
Charon, Mahaf, whose sight is behind him—
that I could take nothing
in my hands, and not even them?

The Second Arrow

I shoot this one. In an artful parabola
it curves over my head and strikes
the gully at my skull's base.

The audience loves it.
They rap their begging bowls
against their walking sticks.

I bow. Blood trickles into my hair.

It's a good trick, and, unexpectedly, repeatable.

Comfort

This is happening to me—
if it were her, I'd ache and rage to trade.

So what I'm living
is somebody's answered prayer.

Red-Eye

Dear country, did you wait for me?
Did you halt yellow trains as they vipered the engineered rural,
did you hinder currents, letting duckweed
slowly lock the waters—have you been a grand museum
of immobile waterfowl and ruminants, flies on their nostrils,
millipede life under leaf rot, stock-still—where it rained,
did glass drops hover in a splintered universe of damp,

dear country, when I dropped the spindle, did you pull the main?
Did you arrest the motions of bicyclists, hooligans,
vendors, classroom chalk scraping in cursive,
the past imperfect—was there a static silence
on all radios?

Here is the private sea scrolling in,
typing you an endless letter. The plane makes its fluid, plummeting turn,
and my window fills with land. Here is the clay
that holds the brittle calcium of them who made me, have they waited—
because I waited for you, in my blind and percolating marrow
all the years I waited, sleepwalking, speaking a daft language flawlessly.

Now the roads are ribbons, and the cars begin to crawl.
I would like to rise with you; I'd like to be so awake.
I've drunk repeated coffees from a small and unbreakable cup
that a child might use to serve tea to a wiry monkey
and a one-eyed bear. But I have left
her in another country, sleeping.
And my hands shake.

Her curls roughen to burlap,
reek of sour milk. Her nails,
small shovels edged with grime,
click and slip against her rainbow abacus,
rhythm of a feral brokerage. No one
takes measure of her shoes, toes crowding
like tree roots; her socks have been damp for days.
Gluey remnants on her cheeks, welts
under the waistband of her tights.
Step stool pushed under the shelf
of walnuts, lentils, apricots,
glandular specimens.
Her grasshopper shirt
is lopsided, it's buttoned all wrong—
would somebody please fix her goddamn buttons?!—
but tenderly, tenderly, kneeling
to be nearer to my grievous spectacle,
my dearest unpossessable.

Hereafter

Then these atoms, held in the aspic of me,
that now like pakoras and Nina Simone,
will loosen in the dark flux,
relinquishing unhurriedly,
and ascend again in rhizomes,
blankly, good as new.

But still will love
this child, somehow
the grasses would love this child.

The Cure for Everything

This, the living do, and I am

capable, goddamnit,
ergo, lento:
plug in drain,
lift bag of salt, cover ears
for the sickening thunder of water.

Existence distilled—undressing
is work, and getting in, unstable limbs
folding, galloping pulse, the surface
a treacherous turbulence of light.

The faucet has two different handles,
whatever was cheapest when they broke. One has five blunted points
and evokes the celestial. The other, six rounded, floral.
They look at me like a loyal animal,
one eye extinguished.

And it's so warm, so warm. And I almost forget to remember what's wrong

I Want to Ride My Bicycle

If there be miracles, then raise me from this bed,
to station racks, urinal and sharpie-scrawled, where warps of spokes
in crowded rows wait for the streaming, convoluted weft of air—
I'll find the frail and sturdy frame that's mine alone, and make
    that intimate
unlocking gesture of release. Return to me the spurs of my winged
    horse,
my whirring bird with her curved shoulders, cogwheel innards,
and one prescient, shining eye. I want to slalom park gates after
    dark,
coast under streetlights as my shadow overturns, a paper doll,
a codex page. I long to push uphill in rainfall, thighs sore, snailing
damp terrain, so near the gutter's sorrel, shepherd's purse, then from
the summit letting all observers blur, the freefall slope that wheels
are faithful to as fingers reading Braille. I want to barrel
through the belly of the Rijksmuseum, vaulted brickwork overhead.
If there be miracles then raise me from this bed.

How to Converse with Bedside Visitors

There you are, in your nimbus of daylight.
Yeah, I feel as spectral as I look.
Report to me in rations—
that world has too much in it,
havoc of ticker tapes.
I've outlived the tiny spider in the upper corner,
who ventured sideways, shadowboxing,
seemed to practice rituals of luck.
Once, I was sure I heard my daughter's voice
downstairs, but it was the plumbing—
still I felt considerably cheered.
I've found that I don't curate
my own past, its episodes projected
in this room. Grade ten
geography class—we were fifteen, why were we
colouring maps? Mr. Ross lived for hockey, punched boys
in the shoulder as greeting, otherwise fiddled with paperclips.
He had a kind of boxy shape, and while he stood
I pictured him as North America:
his breast pocket was Hudson's Bay, his belt
the world's longest so-called
undefended border, and then his penis
of Florida, peeing Keys, his tapered
Mexican legs, and the palindrome
of his shoes—*a man, a plan, a canal: Panama.*
It comforts me when spring rains clatter
on the corrugated roof—hundreds of typewriters,

doing the work I can't do.
The poems I've pasted to walls
peel off, but leave traces, Basho wrote.
Tell me of your life without evasions.
Some days it seems improbable
that there aren't hundreds of me,
at large in rubber boots.

On Giving

Some days, all I have for her
is the ladle of my body
fallen still.

Mineral, Mirabel, Miracle

My friend brings a remedy.

It is the rabbit's corpus callosum.

It is yarrow flower, tissue salts,

spring woods in dark bottles,

moss in an eye dropper's stem.

Our evidence is the unspoken,

steeped in maternal inflections.

I trust her handwritten hair,

her methods of resurrection.

O world, O Welt,
you go on so near,

I can hear your diligent machinery,
axles and sneezes and thoughts,

my friends remember or forget,
they proceed, they play board games, they make new life,

and some come over, afraid
but forcing themselves to be good,

and I get to know their brave, apologetic features
adjusting to the dark,

as they bring their sweaty,
holding hands, their hesitant words,

and take home their private relief, their reports.
Everyone is allowed to breakfast on my misfortune.

All of us at some instance
have to be that one.

Solidarities of Sick Mothers

We find each other through our shoulders; the gesture of squaring them.

Words, we know as generative, obliterating entities.

Through some of them, we live.

With our ears to the ground, by the skin of our teeth, the truth is.

Sour grease of the last remaining pay-phone.

From its dangling receiver: dirges, relatives.

We trade in steaming parcels from our diasporic kitchens.

For our children, we'll kill.

The only reading that we practice is essential.

When one of us throws the match, we cheer her still.

Formation of a Dragonfly

Grotesque
beetle thing, found
in the campfire ashes
at sunrise. We perch it
on a stalk, ask after its name.
The answer
takes hours.
From a hole
in its back,
a curled,
translucent,
somehow larger
body rises.
Wings
of damp fabric;
they unglue
and rise to cruciform.
Black bands
appear at their apices.
The new legs are barbed
with hair. Blunt
bottom lengthens
telescopically
to a slender curve.
Cockpit head. The thorax
darkens with pigment. A pattern
of parallel lines

expands from the abdomen's
side to front,
and a line of is it yellow?—
yes, bright yellow—
draws along a spine
that is, of course,
no spine.
A wind stirs the skin of the lake.
There was a mother,
earlier, but none of this
required her.

In the Country of My Convalescence

Almost my favourite part was the ending.
Tulips, I think, are loveliest then,
losing their duplicate symmetries;

they were nameless when oval and cheerful, clear chorus—
now they declare themselves,
forged in slow fire.

The skins of raw silk involute.
One bloom shuts like the plates of the skull,
another performs a surrendered lament.

The pistils uncloak, they were there all along,
but what flew through this room,
what voice from a whirlwind seeking form?

House of God

That was my cramped apartment when I studied medicine,
and the alarm each morning roused a dread in me
I could not shake or name. I'd rise. I'd muster courage
from a baseboard that I loved because its edge seemed made
of light, even on overcast days; vaporous as chalk dust,
snow blowing from a ridge of snow—like the light
under Diego's chair, in *Sunday Morning #2*.

There was a spare hour. I shadowed a Reiki healer
at his clinic. He asked me to hover my hand
above the patient, who nodded from the table.
My palm prickled as over club soda, then warmed, then followed
the voltaic streams, until at her liver the signal
got lost. *Cirrhosis*, nodded the instructor, overturning
what I thought a body was.

The light under the figure in the chair,
I should have said, or the child on the left,
because Jack Chambers didn't name his youngest son
in that lucent, aquatic work. The same year,
he painted *Victoria Hospital*, a building like a void
under the stark, immeasurable sky. Bleak colours
of an urban winter. He began and would end in that place.
In the foreground, a cluster of bare trees I still swear
are hiding a deer, a coyote, a life.

Then I forgot. The material called. Internal
medicine: creatinine, hematocrit, clostridium difficile. One man
on the ward was near his end. He had the sheer cheeks
and sparse words of my late grandfather, who wore pale suits,
smoked a seafarer's pipe. Seemed to sit for decades,
tabernacled, in one chair. And then we were pallbearers.

This patient thanked me every day
for nothing, really, for practicing my auscultation
on the cavern of his ribs. I was on call
the night his breath began to sound submerged.
I phoned the family, then asked the nurse
what I should do. *Take his vitals*, she said, so I placed
two fingers on his inner wrist, and felt his pulse emit
a slipshod effort, and then stop, and in the room
it was as if a wave receded to the ocean, over pebbles,
over stones that clattered with their consonants,
and then I wept, although I knew I was supposed to listen
for the silence in his chest, and check his pupils
with a light, and make a closing entry in the chart.

The attending was kind. He did
what I should have done. Then he spoke to me
at the nursing desk, this slender man who may have seen
a hundred people die—*All losses are one*, he said
without a reprimand, and a muscle twitched behind his glasses.

Should I tell you the dreams
I had in that apartment? I dreamed a ghost
was sitting round the corner from the bed;
I heard it breathe, I heard the rustling

of the newspaper it read, and when I forced myself
to turn and look, the box of human bones I had
for study was suspended in the air.

It became who I was for that month, as we stood
at the bedsides, with clipboards and styrofoam cups—
their white rims, also, fogging and diffusing,
below the tired murmur of our words. One resident
knew all the opiates cold; generic and brand names and doses.
Another loved to try out new procedures. A third
had been disciplined, something to do with potassium.
And I was the one who'd mistaken the figure for the familiar,
and cried *Diego, Diego, Diego.*

On Industry

I've sensed sunrise at my pillow's edge,
groped for shaded glasses.
Held my child.
I've blessed her day. And I have been supine and mute
until the hours were spun wool, have waited still,
then lifted leaden feet,
traversed the room, for the sake
of movement itself, the effort that refuses
to forsake. I've contemplated
silver flecks that float in turmeric and honey tea.
I have collected supper at my door.
Crept into bed,
then held my child again,
archaically tired and pleased somehow,
like one who has pushed beans into the ground all day,
and knows it could rain or not rain.

Reparations

I take her out for sushi.
The table's an ocean. The table's a crater.
She exerts her trainer chopsticks.
The waiter asks after our water.

I buy her the doll that pees
and crawls. There's a switch in the chest.
She changes her diaper solemnly,
and bandages her head.

I invite the whole class to her party,
craft games from the book of gnomes.
She hides in the rental gym's corner,
emerges much taller and older—

mother, I was alone,
she says, *in all our old haunts,*
at a loss for what I had done or not done
to make you disappear.

The Mother Shirt

My selves hang like shirts
that were skins—

now I am raw and peaceful.
Life washes over me elementally,

wave after wave. Idle sleeves.
The writing shirt

has a crumpled note
in its pocket,

but the ink has bled, illegible blue.
The nostalgic shirt

is embroidered, becoming. The scared
one still quakes,

damp under the arms.
The mother shirt is magnificent,

stained with blackberries and tempera paint.
Oh, but it moves! There is

someone in it, small limbs straining
in the membrane trap.

I pull it over her head and we laugh,
falling on the bed together,

sweet eruption
that goes on a little too long,

like the signal after the slow, shuttered train has gone.

NOTES

The italicized "he wrote" sections in 'Reading dèr Mouw After Bedtime' are from J.A. dèr Mouw's collected sonnets.

The title 'Women Do This Every Day' is from Lillian Allen's 'Selected Poems' of the same name.

The title and italicized lines of 'The Roaring Alongside' are from Elizabeth Bishop's poem 'The Sandpiper'.

The Etty Hillesum citation in 'Paradise Found' is from her collected works.

'Incantation' is for T.A.

'It's the Inner Harbour neighbourhood…' is for L.S.K.

'Mineral, Mirabel, Miracle' is for K.G.

ACKNOWLEDGEMENTS

My enduring gratitude to all the generous people who were there. Each of your gestures lives in me.

Thank you, my dear Villanelles.

I am grateful to Carmine Starnino for his enthusiasm and editorial gifts, and to all at Véhicule Press.

'Red Eye' and 'Incantation' appeared in *The Walrus*. 'Red Eye' was also included in *The Best of Canadian Poetry 2019*, and was a finalist for a National Magazine Award. 'Hereafter', in Dutch translation, was longlisted for the Turing Prize. 'The Imaging Department' won, and 'O Death' was a finalist in, *Arc Poetry Magazine's* Poem of the Year contest. 'Women Do This Every Day' was a finalist in *Briarpatch's* Writing in the Margins contest. 'It's the Inner Harbour Neighbourhood…' was a finalist for the Frontier Industry Prize. 'House of God' received an Honourable Mention in the *Bellevue Literary Review's* Marica and Jan Vilcek Prize for Poetry. Many thanks to the people behind all of these poetry venues.

This work was funded by the Ontario Arts Council, the Canada Council for the Arts, and the Al Purdy A-Frame Residency.

Signal
EDITIONS

Carmine Starnino, Editor
Michael Harris, Founding Editor

Véhicule Press